A souvenir guide

Packwood House

Warwickshire

National Trust

Welcome to Packwood

On 29 September 1904 Alfred Ash, second generation industrialist and confirmed suburban dweller, bought at auction the Packwood estate of approximately 52 hectares (134 acres). When asked why he had done it, he is reported to have said: 'I bought it because the Boy wanted it.'

The 'Boy' was his only son, Graham Baron Ash (1889–1980), who was just 16. For the next 40 years Baron Ash, as he liked to be known, was to be the meticulous restorer, furnisher, decorator and beautifier of Packwood, creating his ideal of the perfect English country house.

Baron Ash

Who was the boy who could inspire his father, an owner of race horses and lover of motor cars, to buy an ancient English manor house? Baron Ash was a complex mix of typically English reserve and true courage, deeply buried emotions and party-loving generosity. His aspirations seem to have masked a degree of social insecurity which surfaced in an almost obsessive concern for correctness in every aspect of life.

Those who knew him portray a kind, fastidious, slightly nervous host and employer. No one has left an intimate memorial of him. It seems possible he didn't permit himself any close relationships.

Work in the family firm of Ash and Lacy was interrupted by the outbreak of war in 1914. Initially Baron Ash volunteered for the medical corps, but in 1917 he transferred to the newly formed Royal Flying Corps to train as a pilot. This was a disaster. Try as he might, he didn't master the art of landing safely and, after wrecking four aircraft, he transferred again, this time to become a Balloon Observation Officer. In this perilous post (observers, suspended under bags of highly flammable gas, were quite defenceless against enemy aircraft), he saw out the war, finding himself in the Belgian city of Tournai as peace was declared.

A passion for antiques

In the strange calm that pervaded the cusp of peace, Baron Ash confided passion to his diary. In the cathedral's Robing Room in Tournai where medieval vestments and tapestries were stored, the boy from Birmingham was amazed: 'I never saw such superb things…there must be at least 50 [copes]…too glorious for words…and entirely covered with silver and gold thread.' Together with the copes and chasubles he saw a very fine set of choir hangings donated to the cathedral in 1402. These must have inspired him, for two days later he bought his first piece of tapestry for Packwood. The tapestry, a 'verdure', now hangs in the Long Gallery.

'A perfect gentleman always'
Horace Stanley, butler at Packwood (1936–39), describing Baron Ash

Above An early morning view of Packwood House, as seen from the road

Right Graham Baron Ash (centre) with his father Alfred (left) and his grandfather Joseph seated around the fireplace in the Entrance Hall at Packwood

Far right Graham Baron Ash, 1917

A world tour

Aged 21, Baron Ash travelled to America, Canada, Japan, Korea, China, Singapore, Burma, India, Egypt, Italy and Switzerland. He kept a diary in which he recorded the cultures he encountered. While at Amoy, he visited a temple 'in order to bribe one of the priests to sell me one of the roof decorations… Although the priests are reputed to be robbers and thieves…this one seemed to have some scruples about parting with [them].' A long life of haggling with antiques dealers had begun.

The Perfect Country House

The house to which Alfred Ash brought his wife, daughter and son to live was a typical Warwickshire manor house with the accretions of centuries lending it a mellow charm.

For Baron Ash, however, the Georgian Gothick windows and Victorian galleried hall, the ivy-covered brick and pervasive render served only to cloud Packwood's Elizabethan perfection. Such later interventions offended his sense of the ideal of a squire's house of Old England. Thus they had to be eradicated and replaced by something more 'authentic' to allow his ideal to emerge.

Son of industry

Such high-minded aesthetic judgements were a million miles from the grafting industry of Baron Ash's origins. His grandfather, Joseph Ash, had set up the firm of Ash and Lacy in 1864 manufacturing perforated zinc wares for industrial and domestic use. The London and North Western Railway was one of his most important customers. The business thrived, providing Joseph's sons with lucrative

Above **Early 19th-century watercolour of Packwood by an unknown artist**

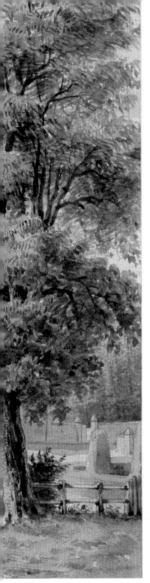

directorships. Alfred Ash succeeded his elder brother as chairman of Ash and Lacy in 1917.

Baron was appointed a director in 1919 but gave up active management soon after in 1922. In January 1935 he resigned from Ash and Lacy, having sold his entire interest in the company, thus cutting all links between his family and the source of its ascent into society. This action can be seen as symbolic of the aspiration Baron had to be a country gentleman. It resembled that of the Fetherston family member, who resided at Packwood House in previous centuries 'in the true style of an English gentleman…clad in the produce of his own estate'.

Alfred, the fun-loving father

Alfred Ash, Baron's father, enjoyed the trappings of wealth in ways that one can imagine caused shivers of embarrassment to his socially sensitive son. Alfred's habit of being driven to the races in a personalised Rolls Royce to witness the performance of one of his horses must have struck the young Baron as loudly ostentatious. His own flirtation with auto-ostentation was extensive, but in a quieter vein, although even he had his new coat of arms emblazoned down the side of the Rolls Royce, personalised number plates affixed and the 'flying lady' on the bonnet illuminated in blue! Certainly his decision taken immediately after his father's death to sell all of his horses suggests that they did not share that particular passion. Nevertheless, they worked together on the transformation of Packwood, father, mother and sister deferring to his creative zeal, until Alfred's death in 1925 left Baron Ash in sole charge of the development of his perfect country house.

Right These photographs of Baron Ash's parents, Alfred and Emily, both date from 1885

'Packwood was…the apple of his eye.'
James Lees-Milne, diarist and first Secretary to the National Trust's Country Houses Committee, 1947

In society

Baron Ash struggled all his life to avoid damning judgements such as James Lees-Milne's (see below). It was his ambition to be seen as a true country gentleman. The industrial origins of his wealth were a fact never to be mentioned. His idyllic country house, perfect in every historical detail and speaking at every turn of his connoisseurship and finely honed taste, would ensure his acceptance into Society. In all outward appearances this ambition was achieved. Baron Ash was even presented at Court.

High Sheriff

Baron Ash also served as High Sheriff for Warwickshire in 1938, turning out in full court dress for the county assizes, with his butler Stanley acting as footman, and trumpeters, with the Ash pennant fluttering from their instruments, there to herald the judge. He hosted the customary High Sheriff's Ball at Packwood where the correspondent of the local newspaper recorded, somewhat breathlessly: 'To stand facing the garden flood-lit with a soft amber light was an unforgettable experience. In the foreground there were large beds of beautiful orange, scarlet and yellow dahlias in masses seldom seen. At the far side…the raised terrace with its herbaceous borders formed a background beyond which was the unique Cromwellian garden of yew trees and box hedges…which stood outlined in the white light which was used with such great effect upon them.'

'He was invariably spruce, dressed in well-ironed lounge suits which betrayed that he was not really a countryman.'

James Lees-Milne, 1947

What's in a name?
Despite the apparent success of his social aspirations, Baron Ash never achieved that social Everest: a title. He inserted his coat of arms along with those of neighbouring families in his Great Hall windows in a bid to claim parity, but the yearning remained. Yet he was blessed with a forename that gave the impression of noble lineage. He always insisted on the use of this second name rather than his first, so perhaps he hoped some would think it was true?

Opposite Graham Baron Ash is shown here as High Sheriff of Warwickshire in this pastel by William Dring, 1943

Left Queen Mary, photographed during her visit to Packwood in 1927

Below Miss Frances Burlison painted this little watercolour in Baron Ash's visitors' book for the High Sheriff's Ball of September 1938

'Really, these bachelors seem to live very comfortably'
HM Queen Mary, 1927

A visit from the Queen

However, the crowning event of Baron Ash's social career had come a decade earlier when, in 1927, he had entertained Queen Mary to tea at Packwood. His work on the house was nowhere near finished, but when the Queen solicited an invitation, it could not to be refused. Despite a torrential downpour at the moment of the Queen's arrival, all went off remarkably well. The visit was memorialised in the preserved cup and saucer from which the Queen took tea (kept ever since that occasion in a small glass case), and the renaming of the room to which she retired to rest. Even in its half-finished state, Packwood had provided the perfect stage for this most treasured marker on the journey from son of industry to established country gentleman that all his life Baron Ash aspired to complete.

Creating antiquity

Between 1924 and 1932 Baron Ash transformed Packwood. His driving ambition to rid the old house of any trace of its Georgian and Victorian inheritance was in tune with the prevailing fashion of the times. The classical style of the 18th century and the dark, heavily furnished interiors of Victoria's reign were deeply unfashionable in inter-war England. A romantic yearning for a time of innocence before the horror of the trenches lit upon the reign of Good Queen Bess – or thereabout – as the mystical prime of Old England. Thence flew the imagination of Baron Ash, with dreams of creating his perfect English country house.

'I am proceeding with the utmost caution. I hope that my efforts will not provide the future with an object lesson of what *not* to do in restoring an old house!'

Baron Ash, *c.*1931

Repairs and some restoration had occupied Alfred Ash and his son for several years before the major restorations were undertaken that changed Packwood so completely. Christopher Hussey recorded in *Country Life* in August 1924: 'The industry and enthusiasm of Mr Ash and his son have…gone far towards repairing the harm wrought by the…unhappy treatment of the place during the latter half of the last century.'

Far more radical changes were to come. Externally one of the biggest was the replacement of all the Georgian Gothick sashes with leaded casements in the Jacobean style. This transformed the place entirely and immediately lent a far more antique appearance to each façade. Nineteenth-century alterations to the line of the gables, particularly on the south (garden) front, were reversed using the evidence of a drawing dating from the mid-18th century.

From cows to queens

Packwood was not a large house. Baron Ash felt the need for a big entertaining room. This, the form of a traditional manor house did not allow. However, the perfect country house of Old England had to have a Great Hall, for feasting, dancing and for general entertaining. What to do? Fortunately an ancient – and large – cow

barn lay close to the manor house, divided from it by only a couple of hundred yards. This he seized upon and, with the addition of a full-height bay window at the head of the hall, the installation of a sprung dancing floor and the conversion of the hay rack as a balustrade for a minstrels' gallery, Baron Ash's Great Hall was born. It was complete for the royal visit in 1927 when the Queen took tea beneath the great bay window in which subsequently, and with permission, her royal arms were installed in stained glass in commemoration of the event.

Above left **Prior to its transformation by Baron Ash, the house featured Gothick sash windows. Behind the large tree you can just glimpse the outline of the cow barn which was to become the Great Hall. This photograph dates from the late 1920s.**

Above right **The west front of the house after the transformation, with its newly created Long Gallery and mass of leaded windows, c.1934–36**

Opposite left **Baron Ash in the bay of the Great Hall; the huge floral arrangement was a typical feature during his time**

Opposite right **The magnificent bay window in the Great Hall**

Left **Charming detail on one of the Great Hall windows**

Architectural salvage

> 'I do this…as an antidote to the decay and demolition of so many old houses all over the country. I am rescuing whatever I can from other places and preserving it here.'
>
> Graham Baron Ash, *c.*1931

The 1920s and 1930s saw much re-use of features from demolished historic buildings. This form of antiquarianism Baron Ash pursued with vigour and great discernment. The fireplace and its plaster overmantel which he installed in the Great Hall came from a vintner's shop in Stratford which may have been known to Shakespeare. Some of the carved heads on the corbels supporting the roof beams are copied from originals in the French town of Carcassonne.

The Entrance Hall was re-modelled, blowing away the cosy galleried staircase hall Baron Ash had inherited by inserting a massive hall window. This grid of glass, lead and wood streams light into the former primly brown

Above **The Entrance Hall**

A plethora of perfect houses

Baron Ash was not alone in his passion for restoring houses to an appearance that had probably never existed historically. Certainly at Packwood there had been neither a Great Hall nor a Long Gallery until Baron Ash created them. Other examples, such as Stoneacre in Kent and Chequers in Buckinghamshire, involved large amounts of speculative re-building. A fascinating restoration with many parallels to Packwood is the Treasurer's House in York. Its owner Frank Green created a Great Hall out of a number of smaller rooms and a Georgian panelled Drawing Room out of two others. Both men were avid collectors of antiques, and both men, during their lifetimes, gave their houses and collections, with detailed instructions as to how they were to be displayed, to the National Trust.

Top left Carved headboard in the Ireton Bedroom. The room is named after the parliamentary general Henry Ireton who is supposed to have slept here

Bottom left Even this radiator is covered with medieval linenfold panelling

Right View from the Great Hall to the Long Gallery

interior. A new staircase was constructed in a wing behind the hall and a new landing, panelled in medieval linenfold, gave access to the bedrooms. Salvage provided panelling to create a screens passage with twin doorways and rare chevron boards for the floor. The boards were rescued from the demolition of Lymore Hall in Wales.

A final flourish

Edwin Reynolds, who had restored Shakespeare's birthplace in Stratford, was employed as architect by Baron Ash. His contributions are quiet and appropriately understated, allowing the salvaged antique material to dominate. However, the final flourish of the great restoration of Packwood came in the form of a Long Gallery in 1932.

It was entirely new, but furnished with salvaged historic panelling and a fireplace, it connects the old house with the new Great Hall. This gave Reynolds the chance to shine, differentiating the new work from that of the house by building boldly in brick with stone dressings. Nikolaus Pevsner, the renowned architectural critic, thought the result looked like a modern grammar school, an insult for which Baron Ash never forgave him – but internally it is a triumph of light and shade, of mellow oak and old tapestry.

Modern comforts were not ignored. The perfect country house had to be kept clean, and vacuum cleaners were purchased for the purpose. A water purifier was installed and running hot and cold water was supplied en suite to all four bedrooms.

Baron Ash the collector

In furnishing his perfect country house, Baron Ash had to find the perfect combination of antique textiles, polished wood, faded gold and *objets extraordinaires* that would convey his ideal of timeless Englishness. In this he proved remarkably skilled, displaying a talent for creating atmosphere. Freshly cut flowers were of the greatest importance, to the extent that he made the provision of them mandatory on handing over Packwood to the Trust in 1941. Photographs and a series of watercolours by his friend Frances Burlison show the warm domesticity he aimed for. Sunlight filtering through ancient stained glass panes in newly-minted windows perfectly harmonised the colours and textures in his beautifully restored country house.

'He…filled it [Packwood] with appropriate furniture, tapestries, stained glass and ornaments of great beauty'

James Lees-Milne, 1947

Essential elements

Two features were crucial to Baron Ash's vision: carved oak and old textiles in the form of tapestry and needlework. Of the former, some was supplied from nearby Baddesley Clinton (see box). Of the latter, Baron Ash bought widely in a field that was then largely unresearched. His earliest purchase of a tapestry, in Tournai at the end of the First World War, was guided by a sense of awe tempered by an innate understanding of what would suit Packwood's traditional rooms. His most celebrated purchase is that of the framed *Judith and Holofernes* in the Hall. This was identified as being made by the short-lived Sheldon tapestry works at Barcheston in Warwickshire. The local nature of its production and its rarity would have appealed to him. Also local were painted hangings. In *Shakespeare's Warwickshire and the Unknown Years*, Oliver Baker, antiques dealer, Shakespearean historian, *bon viveur* and great friend of Baron Ash, maintained that painted hangings, as a cheap alternative to woven ones, were a particular product of Warwick and Birmingham in the 16th and 17th centuries. Again, the local – and Shakespearean – nature of these hangings would have encouraged Baron Ash to buy the set now in Queen Margaret's Bedroom.

Opposite left A view of the Study from the Inner Hall

Opposite right The 19th-century century lacquer chest in the Long Gallery

Above A regular guest at Packwood, artist Frances Burlison created wonderfully evocative watercolours of the house

Above right This ornate cupboard with bone and mother-of-pearl inlay is from Baddesley Clinton

Keeping it local

Baron Ash maintained good relations with his near neighbours at the ancient moated manor house of Baddesley Clinton. He was aware his friend, Cecil Ferrers (1887–1947), was unable to fund the maintenance of the old house so, when the opportunity arose, he bought a handful of items from Baddesley to furnish Packwood. Amongst tapestries, carvings and furniture perhaps the most prominent piece is the magnificent hall table with its distinctive run of massively scrolled central supports. On a slightly bizarre note, he acquired a sedan chair, complete with dummy occupant in the form of an articulated artist's model. Indirectly, Baron Ash rescued Baddesley once more when his sister and niece, part-heirs to his estate, provided a financial endowment that allowed the National Trust to acquire Baddesley Clinton just a few months after Baron Ash's death in February 1980.

Entertaining at Packwood

Parties at Packwood were legendary. In the era of the Jazz Age invitations were sent as ragtime lyrics. Christmas was always the excuse for a vast gathering with quantities of excellent food and drink and numbers of guests counted and recorded carefully in the visitors' books. Even wartime austerity did not stint Baron Ash's generosity. These precious volumes contain the signatures of every visitor to Packwood from 1906 to the year Baron Ash left. What makes them particularly attractive is the number of small drawings and watercolours illustrating life at Packwood that enlivens the catalogue of names. One of the most prolific authors of these was the sculptress Frances 'Bessie' Burlison, the most constant of Baron Ash's guests. Her views of Packwood, its gardens and its people, are most evocative of the era.

Staff at Packwood

Such entertaining needed a dedicated staff to ensure everything ran smoothly. Nevertheless, staffing levels were not high. In 1935 there were five indoor staff and seven outdoors. The butler

Right This page for the 15 April 1935 in the visitors' book shows a delightful illustration of the performance of *All's Well That Ends Well* at the Shakespeare Festival which took place on that day

Far right Concert programme decorated by Frances Burlison

doubled as valet. Even so, everything had to be just right; half measures were not acceptable. For the Queen's visit all was open to royal scrutiny – from the damask of the tablecloth to the curtains in Queen Margaret's Bedroom. Feverish activity had preceded the visit; a rug had been laid over a damp patch in the garden to save the royal shoes. Despite being a demanding employer he was also a generous one and the staff Christmas party was a jolly affair when jokes were played on senior staff – though not, of course, on Baron Ash himself.

Packwood's Follies

Concerts and plays in the Great Hall and in the gardens were a recurring feature and were known collectively as 'Follies'. Theatrical productions on the terrace were the occasion of great parties and further artistic endeavours in the visitors' books. Perhaps the greatest party of all was the High Sheriff's Ball given at Packwood in September 1938 when the band of the Coldstream Guards serenaded

Who signed the spinet?

The visit of the glamorous socialite, Prince George Chavchavadze, caused ripples in local society. He was a White Russian – as the supporters of the deposed Russian monarchy were known – and his recital on the late 17th-century spinet in the Great Hall at Packwood was the hot ticket of the season of 1931. He signed the instrument, which is now in the Drawing Room. It was also the occasion of the first meeting of Baron Ash with James Lees-Milne of the National Trust, which was to have momentous repercussions for the future of Packwood.

over 300 guests while they enjoyed caviar, foie gras and iced pea soup. The floor in the Great Hall was sprung especially for dancing.

'A very good host, he loved entertaining (his food was always delicious)'

James Lees-Milne, 1947

Above **Prince George Chavchavadze** playing the spinet, as depicted by Frances Burlison

Far left Shakespeare's *Henry V* by Frances Burlison, 18 September 1937

Left The Warwick Pageant painted by Frances Burlison, July 1930

Packwood for the nation

On 30 June 1941, Baron Ash gave Packwood, its collections, park and garden and £30,000 to the National Trust in memory of his parents. It came as a shock to everyone. Even his only sister, whose home it had been up until her marriage, knew nothing of it until she heard it on the radio. Why did he do it? He left no record, but some conclusions can be drawn from his instructions on how Packwood was to be kept and presented.

In his 'Memorandum of Wishes' he stated: 'No addition shall be made to the furniture… but the furniture and effects placed in position

'If one stayed a night at Packwood and left a book lying on a downstairs table it would be removed a minute after one quitted the room…he hated disorder.'

James Lees-Milne, 1947

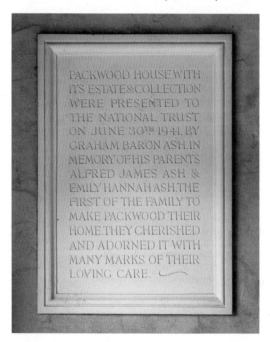

PACKWOOD HOUSE WITH ITS ESTATE & COLLECTION WERE PRESENTED TO THE NATIONAL TRUST ON JUNE 30TH 1941. BY GRAHAM BARON ASH, IN MEMORY OF HIS PARENTS ALFRED JAMES ASH & EMILY HANNAH ASH, THE FIRST OF THE FAMILY TO MAKE PACKWOOD THEIR HOME. THEY CHERISHED AND ADORNED IT WITH MANY MARKS OF THEIR LOVING CARE.

and handed over by me shall be kept in position in which I shall place them…and the National Trust shall make every effort…to give the appearance that the rooms are actually lived in and that flowers shall be provided.'

He had perfected his ideal country house and now there was nothing left for him to do. Besides, he had fallen in love with a ruin in Suffolk. After an interval as the National Trust's tenant at Packwood, he left for Wingfield Castle in 1947.

So long as Packwood was maintained as he instructed – and precisely as he instructed

Above **The Long Gallery fireplace flanked by tapestries**

Left **Memorial plaque in the porch**

Above **The clock in Queen Mary's Bedroom**

– it would remain as his legacy to posterity; a meticulously restored country house of Old England. Ironically, the care and precision with which Baron Ash arranged the house for public visiting ironed out the peculiarities of his living there, the personal touches that would have made the place specific to him. Instead he left what he perceived to be 'correct' country house arrangement – as seen in the pages of magazines like *Country Life* – which had precisely the effect of driving out those qualities of individuality he wished to preserve. James Lees-Milne's description of Packwood sums up the effect of Baron Ash's arrangement: 'If Packwood House looks an immaculate museum today, it was an immaculate museum when Baron lived in it. It

was never a proper country house, with worn hats and tobacco pouches in the Hall, dogs' baskets and children's toys in the living rooms. Heaven forbid! Baron would have died of horror at the very idea.'

Staying true

The National Trust is as faithful to Baron Ash's wishes as possible; flowers are provided in season and the arrangement of rooms varies for practical or conservation reasons only. This policy of presentation makes the addition of homely touches such as a pair of slippers in the hearth or a croquet mallet by the door impossible; such would be untrue to Baron Ash. A visit to Packwood is a journey round the private dream of a singular man.

Packwood before Ash

The Fetherston family owned land at Packwood from the 15th through to the middle of the 19th century. In about 1570, William Fetherston built a new 'great mancient howse'.

In 1599 it was made over to William's son John, when it is first recorded. The house John inherited was tall, detached and nearly square in plan, with triple gables and a great brick cow barn to the north with further farm buildings to the east. The house would have looked similar to how it appears in the anonymous sketch made of the south front in 1756.

A farming dynasty

The Fetherstons were yeoman farmers. Each generation expanded the estate through industry. John Fetherston II (d.1670),

son of John Fetherston, was a lawyer by whom the family's wealth increased greatly. He built the stables and outhouses with their complex brickwork, cupolas and many sundials. His son, Thomas, could afford to take the onerous duty of High Sheriff for the county when called upon to do so in 1692. At his death in 1714 he commanded an estate of around 280 hectares (690 acres).

This was the highpoint of the Fetherston family fortunes. Through the 18th century, succession through the female line carried Packwood to the Leigh family and then to the Dilkes who were responsible for putting in the Gothick sashes and covering the half-timbering under a layer of render. The last of the line died in comparative poverty, with Packwood leased and eventually sold in 1869 to George Oakes Arton, a Birmingham solicitor. George died in 1901

JOHN FETHERSTON, of Packwood House, in the County of Warwick, Esq[r] F.S.A.

The County View of PACKWOOD House of the County of Warwick.

Thomas Fetherston Leigh Esq[r]

and his wife and family moved to Bournemouth, thus hastening the decline of the property. In 1902, *Country Life* could describe 'ancient walls, vested with ivy, clinging to them sometimes in too fond an embrace…its very trunks have crept through the walls'.

By then the principal interest of the property was not in the house. *Country Life* had travelled 'the lane [that] wound among fat and tuneful meadows…' not to see the half-timbered mansion of the Fetherstons, but to revere the celebrated and, by then, mystical antiquity of the gardens.

Above The gate to the Yew Garden in 1868

Opposite left Framed coat of arms of John Fetherston

Opposite right The South Front about 1756, before the half-timbering was covered up

A Garden to Dream In

The garden that Alfred Ash bought at Packwood was already famed for its antiquity and its atmospheric charm.

Country Life had opined that 'England would be richer if it possessed a greater number of gardens like those of Packwood, speaking of the taste and spirit of former times.' Despite the garden's lack of maintenance, the article noted the peculiarities of its architecture, its mellow brickwork, the 'quaintly beautiful garden steps…ingeniously built of wedge-shaped bricks', the beauty of the wrought iron and the oddity of the bee boles in the terrace wall.

The bones of the garden

All these elements and the basic form of the garden were indeed ancient. John Fetherston II was responsible for laying out the architecture of the garden in the late 17th century with a raised brick terrace running parallel to the south front of the house and united to it by brick walls punctuated at the four angles by gazebos, summer houses and a banqueting house. Beyond it, to the south seems to have

Above The double borders in the Carolean Garden, looking towards the Terrace Borders and the Yew Garden

been an orchard and, even at this early date, the beginnings of a topiary garden.

In 1927 the garden designer Geoffrey Jellicoe wrote about its charms. To him, and by this date many others, the garden had assumed an aura of mysticism that was at the very essence of Englishness and – suitably vaguely – religion. 'Packwood is essentially English,' he wrote. 'It has that want of a complete unified plan…that seems to characterise English work… Above all, it has a worldliness combined with a curious, vague, indefinable mysticism that seems to be somehow inherent in the northern race.' It was the Yew Garden that had particularly captured his imagination (see pages 22–23).

'Not anywhere have we found anything more quaint and beautiful than the old gardens at Packwood House'

Anon. *Country Life*, 1902

The Yew Garden

'…where the Sermon on the Mount is…represented in clipped yew. At the entrance to the mount…stand four tall yews…for the four evangelists, and six more on either side for the twelve apostles. At the top of the mount is an arbour formed in a great yew-tree, called the pinnacle of the temple'

R. Blomfield and F.I. Thomas, *The Formal Garden in England*, 1892

Thus the story was related to Blomfield 'by the old gardener who was pleaching the pinnacle of the temple', and is the first recorded instance of it. However, the form of the garden is much older. The mount and the apostles and evangelists appear on a plan of 1723. A further century or so elapsed before 'the multitude' – as the scattering of yews leading up to the mount was christened – was planted by one of the tenants of Packwood in the 1850s. It is only in the 1868 sale catalogue for the property that the Yew Garden is first mentioned in print. Yet within the space of a generation its antiquity and mystical

associations were firmly established.

Whether or not religious associations were in the mind of John Fetherston when he laid out the mount and its transverse terrace plantings is not recorded. Certainly the period was one in which the Church dominated peoples' lives. Mysticism attached itself to gardening as it did to other arts. Ralph Austen published *The Spiritual Use of a Garden* in 1652, in which he quotes a clergyman visiting his garden, 'I seldome come to your garden but… your trees speak something of Christ and the Gospel.'

To create walks in a garden with 'the Hedges cut and Trees pruned and nailed and not an irregular Twig left' was thought to imitate the actions of God who 'is careful to preserve the Garden of his Church in all decency and order.' (William Waller, *Divine Meditations*, 1680)

Modern challenges

The age of the yews and their massive scale provides challenges for today's gardeners. It takes two gardeners, with assistance from volunteers, two-and-a-half months using hydraulic hoists to clip the yews, some of which are over 15 metres high. The box hedging that borders the garden is a riotous amorphous mass, in stark contrast to the stately elegance of the conical topiary. Poor drainage compounded by compaction makes the trees susceptible to disease. Over the coming years it is hoped that a programme of severely cutting back 50 per cent of the yew trees will help to re-invigorate them.

Topiary in context

Topiary gardens of the 17th century, like Packwood, are rare in England. The Best Garden at Chastleton in Oxfordshire (pictured), although replanted since the 17th century, retains the circular plan and clipped form of the yews. At Levens Hall in Cumbria a massive array of topiarised yew and box was laid out in the late 17th century. The resurgence of interest in topiary in the 19th century, led by William Barron the innovative Head Gardener at Elvaston Castle in Derbyshire, was due to the influence of these ancient romantic survivals.

The borders and the mingled style

Photographs and watercolours show that Baron Ash – or rather his Head Gardener, Mr Weaver – crammed the terrace and wall borders with every variety of flower, aiming at strong and lasting expanses of colour throughout the seasons. This approach to planting was coined by Victorian horticulturalist John Claudius Loudon as the 'mingled style'.

The great mass of flowers burgeoning from the Yellow Border and on the Terrace in numerous photographs and paintings show the skill and success of Mr Weaver. Dennis Lindup succeeded to the post and continued the tradition. Graham Stuart Thomas, the National Trust's Gardens Adviser, described his way of working: 'He plants in very small groups, so that when a plant has given its best there is not a large gap left. Many small popular flowers are used…which give a brilliant effect when seen along the length of the wall.'

Above This border beautifully demonstrates the abundant planting so typical of Packwood

Opposite left The Terrace Border in August, with its vibrant mix of rudbeckias, heleniums and salvias

Dennis Lindup retired in 1981 but the mingled style has been carried on and developed by his successors. The labour-intensive nature of the style, with many small groups of plants which require replacement as soon as they have flowered, means it is hard to maintain. As garden writer and photographer Tony Lord observed in his book *Best Borders* (1994): 'Throughout the summer the tiniest patch of bare soil is regarded as the most reprehensible of faults.'

Top right Sunflowers, heleniums, *Geranium palmatum* and *Lythrum salicara*

Above right In August, grasses add grace and movement to the double borders in the Carolean Garden

'The great art…in this kind of flower-border is to employ such plants as produce…masses of flowers; and such a variety in regard to time of flowering as may afford some of every colour in flower from February to October'

John Claudius Loudon, *Encyclopaedia of Gardening*, 1822

Extending the tradition

While maintaining what Fred Corrin, the previous Head Gardener, described in the Yellow Border as the 'unrestrained mix of flowers reminiscent of a cottage garden writ large', the current Head Gardener, Mick Evans, has introduced tender shrubs and other perennials to the mix in the narrow Terrace Borders. Even so, the strong rhythm of planting in groups repeated down the border that is one of the defining features of the mingled style continues to dominate, but without the strict height gradations of Loudon's system. Random plant heights in the narrow depth of these borders give a greater sense of abundance while allowing for the longer season that Loudon aimed for.

Staking was always essential to keep such an abundance of different flowers upright and stable. In spring a sloping plane of brushwood is laid along the length of the Yellow Border through which the riotous herbaceous mix then grows and by which it is supported.

The new mingled style

Innovative features of this 'new mingled style' include placing the borders within the context of their surroundings rather than letting them stand as isolated incidents entirely self-contained. Imperial purples and reds in the Terrace Borders respond to the deep burgundy shades of copper beech trees in the park and the warm tones of the 17th-century brick add movement and depth to blooms of hot orange and tawny red.

The new double border that lines the axial path across the South Lawn develops the sense of rhythm and colour of the mingled style with height offered by grasses and silver colouring to act as a foil to the repeated plantings of cardoon and purple loosestrife. Seen against the looming black-green mass of

Above **The Sunken Garden**

the yew giants beyond, it is highly dramatic.

Over the lawn lies an enclosed Sunken Garden, a typically Arts and Crafts creation that was cut short by wartime austerity in 1941. Breathing new life, Mick Evans has planted it as a dry garden on a bed of crushed brick with exotic desert plants interspersed with hot orange and red low-lying flowers so that the conceit of the formal sunken garden, hidden behind its yew walls, remains.

'a changing tapestry of plants…best apprehended at close range'

Tim Richardson, *The New English Garden*, 2013

The garden courts

Left The approach to the house, as Baron Ash conceived it, is through these ornate gates which frame the building and lead you towards the entrance

Right Packwood's unusual plunge pool

To the west an avenue had been planted by the end of the 17th century to give a formal approach to the house. A plunge pool or cold bath was constructed by Thomas Fetherston in about 1680 in what he called his Fountain Court (now the North Court). He planted holly hedges around it both to supplement brick walls for modesty and as a drying ground. Linen could be laid over the hedges using the spikey leaves of the holly to hold everything in place.

As part of his improvements in 1927–32, Baron Ash constructed a new approach to the house entering off the lane through new gates to the north and following round the new Great Hall to the west front. This necessitated the creation of a North Court, screening the offices with a new wall. On the corner he planted yew topiaries of a fox, a dog and a bird, none of which survive. It is this view that Nikolaus Pevsner condemned as looking like a grammar school. An orchard and wildflower meadow offer informal relief between the formality of the West Court and Fountain Court.

The East Court by which visitors enter Packwood today had long been the everyday entrance to the house. Its domestic scale heralds the amiable rusticity of the house beyond. However, this is immediately challenged by the massive hall window inserted by Baron Ash to the right of the porch which seems to belong to another building altogether. Spires of tree echium compete to bring it back to the scale of the house while a fig curls carelessly over the fancy brickwork of John Fetherston's domestic range. Opposite the gates and across the road, an avenue to match that on the west seems to have been planted in the early 19th century stretching out to the eastern boundary of the estate.

Keeping time

John Fetherston seems to have harboured a particular affection for sundials; there are four wall dials on the outbuildings at Packwood, all differently orientated, and a standard one in the West Court which bears the date 1667. Sundials provided the most reliable form of time-keeping before the invention of clocks. John Fetherston was particularly keen on dials that incorporated mottoes. The one on the stables faces west and is inscribed *Sine septem horis* (meaning 'seven without the hours') denoting that on the longest day it will tell all but seven of the hours of sunshine.

The Kitchen Garden

A walled enclosure, probably acting as a kitchen garden, was in existence by 1723. The Fetherstons would have aimed at virtual self-sufficiency with dairy and meat from the farms of the estate, fish from the Great Pool in the park and fruit and vegetables from the walled garden. The flue that heated the walls of the main south border in the Carolean Garden was installed to protect early blossom of fruit such as peach and apricot. This suggests that fruit may have been grown throughout the garden wherever there was a south or south-westerly aspect.

The walled form of the Kitchen Garden seems to have expanded and contracted throughout history; the present low wall at the south end being a later alteration allowing longer hours of evening sun in summer to warm the crops.

The current Kitchen Garden owes much to the vision of the gardening team and a band of dedicated volunteers. The plan is based on an 18th-century estate map. Vegetables are planted in rows in beds around a central circular pool. Traditional rotation of crops is observed for best results and the produce is often to be found on the menu of Packwood's café. Fruit is grown on espaliers. The garden is staffed almost entirely by volunteers.

Right Divided into quadrants by neatly trimmed box hedges, the Kitchen Garden is home to a cutting border, fruit trees and row upon row of vegetable and salad crops

Contemporary touches

Although it follows a traditional form, the Kitchen Garden does offer a few surprises. You may find a champagne bottle in a tree – a reference to the glamorous 20th-century history of Packwood – or a little gable housing pots containing little garden musings. And the odd Wellington boot might be used as a signpost.

A Lasting Legacy

'A House to dream of, a Garden to dream in'

Margaret Williams, Packwood Visitors' Book, 1 October 1934

Baron Ash was no coward. His experiences of the First World War stand testimony to that. Yet, in tune with the society in which he lived, he spent the two decades following it in headlong flight from its memory. For him this meant enveloping himself in the warmth of nostalgia, creating a sepia-tinted world all of his own. In this world everything was in its place, everything was ordered as it should be, perfect and of great beauty and with a long history. His learning was extensive, so that he could surround himself with all the trappings of country life without ever having to experience the reality of it. In this dream-like world he could throw parties for the county, converse knowledgably with connoisseurs and live his fantasy of the life of the English country gentleman.

Then another war loomed and his perfect world had to move. Despite offering his services to the RAF, he was soon designing a new future, even further retired from reality, in a moated medieval castle in deepest Suffolk which he leased, restored and furnished. Here he remained, creating a new historical fantasy, decorated with newly acquired treasures, but never owned. Thus it is his first-born, the 'apple of his eye' at Packwood that remains his epitaph. It is with Packwood that Baron Ash, the heir to an industrial fortune, made his statement of his belief in the ancient hierarchies of England and it is with Packwood that he made his bid to leave his signature on its rural heart.

Illustration in Packwood Visitors' Book by Margaret Williams, 1 October 1934